SCHIRMER'S LIBRARY
OF MUSICAL CLASSICS

Vol. 12

Johann Sebastian Bach

A L B U M

Of Twenty-One Favorite Pieces

For the Piano

Arranged and Edited by

SARA HEINZE

ISBN 0-7935-5240-0

G. SCHIRMER, Inc.

DISTRIBUTED BY

HAL•LEONARD®
CORPORATION
7777 W. BLUEMOUND RD. P.O. BOX 13819 MILWAUKEE, WI 53213

CONTENTS

13670

Gavotte.

(From the Fifth French Suite.)

J. S. BACH.

Menuet.

(From the First Partita.)

D. C. al Fine.

Passepied.

(From the Fifth English Suite.)

Allegretto vivace.

D.C. al Fine.

Sarabande.

(From the Fifth English Suite.)

Gavotte.

(From the Sixth English Suite.)

10

D. C. al Fine.

Sarabande.

(From the First French Suite.)

Bourrée.

(From the Second English Suite.)

Molto allegro.

Fine.

D.C. al Fine.

Gigue.

(From the First Partita.)

Allegretto espressivo e con moto.

Präludium.

(From the First Partita.)

Menuet.

(From the Third French Suite.)

Poco allegro.

10.

D. C. al Fine.

Gavotte.

(From the Third English Suite.)

Fine.

D.C. al Fine.

Aria.
(From the Fourth Partita.)

Allegretto.

12.

Bourrée.

(From the Third Suite for 'Cello.)

D. C. al Fine.
senza repetizione.

Bourrée.

(From the Suite for Trumpet.)

Intrata.
(From the Fifth Suite for 'Cello.)

Bourrée.

(From the Second Violin-Sonata.)

Rondo-Gavotte.
(From the Sixth Violin-Sonata.)

Allegretto e giocoso.

Préambule.
(From the Sixth Violin-Sonata.)

Arr. by Sara Heinze

Allegro molto e con brio

J. S. Bach

Menuet.

(From the First Suite for 'Cello.)

Aria.

"My Heart ever faithful."

(From the Pentecost-Cantata.)

Gavotte.

(From the Sixth Suite for 'Cello.)

Allegro moderato.

21.

D. C. al Fine
senza repetizione